DUD

& PETE

The Dagenham Dialogues

Peter Cook and Dudley Moore

drawings by Bert Kitchen
photographs by Lewis Morley

D0242734

A Methuen Paperback

A Methuen Paperback

First published in Great Britain 1971
by Methuen and Co Ltd
This paperback edition published 1988
by Methuen London Ltd
11 New Fetter Lane, London EC4P 4EE
Copyright © 1971 by Peter Cook and Dudley Moore

Printed in Great Britain
by Richard Clay Ltd, Bungay, Suffolk

British Library Cataloguing in Publication Data

Cook, Peter
  Dud & Pete: the Dagenham dialogues. –
  (A Methuen humour classic).
  I. Title II. Moore, Dudley
  828'.91407

  ISBN 0-413-53770-6

The cover photographs are from 'Not Only But Also' copyright
BBC Enterprises 1988.

DUD & PETE
The Dagenham Dialogues

PETE. I think it was rightly said, 'See Dagenham Dye Works and die'.

DUD. Yes, but think of all the happy times you've had. That's what I do when I'm feeling below par. This room is filled with joyous memories. Look at this. A certificate proving we've been up the Post Office Tower.

PETE. And why did we go up it?

DUD. Because it was there, Pete, a challenge.

PETE. A brief escape from a life consisting of cups of tea, interminable games of Ludo and the occasional visit to your Aunt Dolly.

DUD. Well, what does this remind you of?
He shows PETE *a souvenir programme.*

PETE. It reminds me of our dismal visit to the Planetarium.

DUD. That was nice, wasn't it? Seeing the sky at night during broad daylight.

PETE. And emerging into a cold wind and drizzle, buying a newspaper only to read the headline 'London Airport Disaster – thirty old ladies sucked to death in Jumbo Jet engine.'

DUD. But think of the millions of old ladies who weren't sucked to death in a jet engine, who are now happily playing snap up and down the country.

PETE. The mental image of millions of old ladies shouting 'Snap' at each other merely confirms my ideas about the futility of life. . . .

Methuen Humour Classics

To

Auntie Beeb
Uncle Lew
Mr & Mrs Woolley
Dr Groarke
Aunt Dolly
Uncle Bert
Joan Harold
Daphne Meacham
Her Most Gracious Majesty
Stella Newby
The Reverend Stephens
Roy Taylor
Mrs McDermott

Contents

Acknowledgements

Eleven of the scripts published in this book were originally transmitted by the BBC in the programme *Not Only But Also*; three of these were subsequently published in *The Listener*. The sketch 'By Appointment' was originally performed as part of the Royal Performance at the Palladium Theatre in 1965.

DUD

& PETE

Caught in the Act

DUD. Tea's up, Pete.

PETE. Shhh.

DUD. What's up?

PETE. Guard your tongue.

DUD. Pardon?

PETE. Do you not realize we are being bugged?

DUD. Bugged?

PETE. Over the last six years we have been constantly monitored by the K.G.B.

DUD. Is that the lemon juice people?

PETE. No, it's the secret service of the Russians. They've taken down every word we've said.

DUD. Mr Woolley might be one of theirs.

PETE. Aunt Dolly may be in on it too . . . it's a conspiracy.

DUD. But why would they want to listen to us?

PETE. My dear Dud, we represent the sophisticated British man . . . it's not unnatural that they should want to delve into the secrets of what makes us tick.

DUD. Who's behind this international conspiracy?

PETE. Yehudi Methuen and Company. Every word we say is taken down and transmitted to Russia.

DUD. Is that really true Pete?

PETE. As the day I was born, Dud.

DUD. Well, what I say is 'Sod 'em'.

PETE. I should withdraw that remark, it'll all go down in their little book.

Superstitions

PETE. Tea's up, Dud.

DUD. Here, did you put the sugar in before the milk?

PETE. Yer, I think so.

DUD. You'd better stand up, close your eyes, turn round twice while I throw this lot out the window.

PETE. What's the point of that?

DUD. It's very unlucky to put the sugar in before the milk, didn't you know that?

PETE. It doesn't make any difference. It tastes just the same.

DUD. It might taste just the same, Pete, but it has terrible effects on your life. You put the sugar in first, that's very unlucky. My Aunt Dolly put the sugar in before the milk one day and over the next forty years she lost all her teeth.

PETE. Is that due to putting in the sugar before the milk?

DUD. It's due to that very thing. Tell you another thing I'm very careful about, Pete, is railings. Whenever I see railings I know I have to count them, otherwise it will be unlucky and something awful will happen to me. For instance when I go up the Merry Fiddlers to have a couple of pints, when I come back, you know the railings that stretch all the way back from the Merry Fiddlers to our front door, I count every one of them. Now the other day, last Friday, I was just getting to number four hundred and ninety-three and I saw Mrs Taylor across the road. I said 'Hello, Mrs Taylor. How are you, Mrs Taylor?' I turned back, I'd lost my place. I thought: I can't risk it, I can't risk going wrong, I've got to buzz back to the Merry Fiddlers and start again.

PETE. How many railings are there, Dud?

DUD. Five hundred and ninety-three.

PETE. It's very interesting it should be *exactly* that number, Dud. If you ask me, there must be something in all this occult business. You remember my Uncle Bert?

DUD. Very vaguely.

PETE. That's how people remember him, very vaguely, my Uncle Bert. Well, one day he was in the kitchen. He'd just finished having tea, you know, like you or me, and he was just about to place the milk in the fridge when suddenly this black cat ran in front of him. Of course, what he should have done is stood on his head, thrown the milk backwards and crossed himself to avoid the evil spirits. Well, he was very late for the pictures so he didn't take any precautions and sure enough seven years, four months and three days later he was run down by a bus.

DUD. That shows you, Pete, you can't ignore the omens.

PETE. You mustn't ignore the omens, no. Of course, Uncle Bert, he used to dabble in the occult, especially during the warm weather. I remember once, it must have been the summer of 1953, a blazing hot afternoon, I just come down the stairs and I went into the sitting room and there was Uncle Bert, sitting there, with all the heavy velvet curtains drawn. You remember those heavy velvet curtains they used to have?

DUD. Very vaguely.

PETE. Well they were drawn, fairly distinctly, and he was sitting there in the dark. So I said, 'I'm sorry to disturb you, Uncle Bert', and he said, 'Oh no, come on in, Pete. I'm looking into the secrets of the future'. So I sat down. He had these amazing tarot cards, you know the tarot cards. He was taking one tarot out after the other, throwing it on the table and predicting the future, it was quite incredible, Dud. He said, 'During the next ten years an amazingly important event will occur.' Sure enough four years later, World War II broke out. And that wasn't the only thing. You want to know what he said as well?

DUD. Yer.

PETE. He said, 'The weather is going to be unpredictable'. He predicted that years before it happened.

DUD. Course you know, Pete, all these superstitions have their origins in the Black Ages when people wandered about in a state of ignorance and unrest.

PETE. Course they did, Dud.

DUD. That was the time when strange spirits were abroad.

PETE. Oh we had some here as well.

DUD. The fear of Lucifer and the dark spirits was in everybody's heart.

PETE. Course it was, Dud. There were lots of witches about in those days. You know about witches, Dud?

DUD. No I don't, Pete.

PETE. In medieval times when they suspected someone of being a witch, Dud, the villagers used to seize hold of her and get lots of string and tie it all round her and they'd attach pebbles what they found in the forest nearby. And then the eldest of the village – well not absolutely the eldest 'cause they were too weak to do it – the *youngest* of the eldest, the sort of middleagest, used to grab hold of the alleged witch and thrust her in the pond. And if she floated, they knew she was a witch and they hauled her out and waited for her to dry off and then they burnt her.

DUD. What did they do if she sunk?

PETE. If she sunk and drowned, that meant she was innocent. Rather a poor deal, they had, the innocent witches.

DUD. Course nowadays you'd be tried by a local magistrate, which would be totally different, wouldn't it?

PETE. Yer, we've come a long way since those unenlightened times.

DUD. Course we have.

PETE. They had no morals in those times.

DUD. We wouldn't have that sort of cruelty would we? Do you know Pete, actually, it's interesting this, 'cause the whole business of the dark regions of the mind has always fascinated me. You remember Mr Woolley?

PETE. No.

DUD. You see, nobody remembers him. Well, during the war, he was in the trenches one day – he was fighting on the front-end – he was polishing his rifle when he suddenly cut his finger on the view-finder, and you wouldn't believe it, three thousand miles away, in Glasgow, his mum, in the middle of the night – woke up in a cold sweat, sucking her thumb, and saying in a voice that was scarcely her own, Pete, 'My little one has been injured, my boy has been damaged.'

PETE. That's telepathy, Dud. That's all it is, telepathy. I'm telepathetic you know, Dud. I can tell what people are thinking. For example you think of something and I'll tell you what you're thinking.

DUD. I bet you can't.

PETE. Course I can. Shut your eyes and think of something.

DUD. All right.

PETE. You thought of anything?

DUD. No I can't think of anything.

PETE. Well think of an apple . . . No don't think of that 'cause I told you. Think of something similar to that.

DUD. I'll try.

PETE. Have you thought of something?

DUD. Yer, yer.

PETE. Right, I'll tell you what it is. I believe you're thinking: 'I bet you can't tell what I'm thinking.'

DUD. How did you know that then? It's uncanny.

PETE. It stood out a bloody mile, Dud. I can read you like

a book, and a bloody boring book it is as well.

DUD. It's amazing you know, Pete, to have those sort of powers. Course, do you ever get the feeling that the hand of a nameless dread is clutching at your heart?

PETE. You mean intimations of unbelievable horror?

DUD. Yer.

PETE. Yer, I get that every afternoon, quite often when I'm coming home from work in the twilight, by dusk, you know, and the street is deserted and I look down and I see the cracks of the pavement and I know full well that if I tread on one of those cracks, a great big bogeyman is going to come out from behind the dustbins and carry me off to his mountain lair and tear me rim from rim.

DUD. That's terrible, Pete. I used to get that very feeling when I was a little boy, 'cause my mum used to say to me when I'd been a little pest, she used to say, 'Dud, don't you dare go near number 49 Leamington Crescent. It's an evil place, don't you ever go near there.' Of course, I was a curious lad and one day . . .

PETE. I remember that at school.

DUD. What?

PETE. I remember that, you were a very curious lad at school.

DUD. Funny you should remember that, Pete. Well anyway, one day after school, I went along to 49 Lymington Crescent – I went with Roy Taylor and Michael Austin. We opened the gate, and we started creeping stealthily up the garden path, which crunched under our feet.

PETE. Crunch, crunch.

DUD. Yer, very similar to that noise you're making now. And then we picked our way stealthily across the lawn, squashing the rotting apples that were lying there and then we came upon this sooty window where cobwebs had accumulated over the centuries and we looked in, fear in our hearts, and we saw Mr Lewis of the hardware store dancing to a suspended kipper.

PETE. Was that a Druid rite, Dud?

DUD. Yer. Perhaps even earlier – a Nordic rite, something like that.

PETE. You know what happened to me once, when I was young?

DUD. What?

PETE. I was in the spinney with Daphne Meacham and suddenly we come across, amidst the pine needles, the form of a dead bat. I'd read something of dead bats in a book of the occult. So naturally I went to my blazer and pulled out a pin, stuck the pin into my finger until the blood ran, then I stuck a pin into Daphne Meacham until the blood ran and then I stuck the pin into the bat until its blood ran and then I got all the running blood together and mingled them. And then for an amazing moment we were all gifted with uncanny powers of hearing. From over the hills from over a mile away, I could here my mother shouting, 'Come on home Pete, the bleeding dinner's going cold.'

DUD. Fantastic.

PETE. Have you ever had a nameless dread of anything?

DUD. I tell you one that keeps me awake day and night Pete. When I go to the lav, I know I've got to get down the stairs before the flush stops going. I know that once that flush has started I've got thirty-five seconds to get down and if I don't get down in time, I will die.

PETE. You don't believe that, do you?

DUD. Course I do.

PETE. That can't be true, Dud, 'cause a lavatory is a modern invention. Superstitions have to date back to medieval times. The lavatory was invented in the eighteenth century by John Louis Stevenson. He was sitting in the bath one day when suddenly he said, 'Eureka, I've thought of the lavatory'. So that superstition can't be true, 'cause it doesn't go back long enough.

DUD. I think it's true Pete, I think it's absolutely true.

PETE. You mean to say if I went up there now, went to the lavatory, pulled the chain and I wasn't downstairs by the time it stopped flushing I'd die?

DUD. Yer.

PETE. A load of cobblers, I'll go up and do it.

DUD. Look, don't mess about, Pete, don't fool around with the fates.

PETE *goes upstairs.*

Come downstairs and finish your tea.

PETE. I'm up here, Dud.

DUD. Pete, come on down. It's dangerous. Don't tamper.

PETE. I'm going to pull the chain, Dud.
He pulls the chain.

DUD. Pete, you've got thirty seconds, come down. NOW Pete, come on down. You haven't got very long.

PETE. I'm not moving. I don't care.

DUD. You'll live to regret it, Pete – or rather you'll die.

PETE. I won't.

DUD. The powers of darkness will be upon you.

PETE. They won't touch me, Dud.

DUD. Pete, come on down, Pete. It's stopped.

PETE. AAAAAARGH!

DUD. Pete what's happened?

PETE. I've crossed the threshold of the dead, Dud; the dark powers have got me, Dud; I'll come and haunt you in the lav, Dud. From the rising of the sun till the going down of the same I shall not forsake thee.

DUD. It didn't count that time, Pete. I had my fingers crossed.

On Music

PETE. Isn't it wonderful?
DUD. Oh it's absolutely glorious, this music.

PETE. Debussy is so brilliant at conjuring up a whole scene with the use of his instruments.

DUD. Yer.

PETE. You can almost see the scene, can't you?

DUD. Yer.

PETE. 'La Mer.'

DUD. Yer.

PETE. There she is – Debussy's mother, comes into the room, a silver tray covered with a silver tea-pot, silver cups . . .

DUD. Silver hair.

PETE. Silver hair on the mother. She comes in – Debussy sitting there on the sofa in his little blue smock – she pours the tea. D'you hear the tea being poured?

DUD. Yer, you can almost hear the cream going into the cup.

PETE. Not too little.

DUD. Not too much.

PETE. Just right. And outside – what is it?

DUD. A bird. A bird twittering its roundelay of summer mirth, Pete.

PETE. The flute takes up the theme of the bird, it's wonderful.

DUD. You can almost see the myriad hues of his feathers.

PETE. Beautiful.

DUD. And mum gets on with the ironing.

PETE. Beautiful.

DUD. The bread baking in the oven.

PETE. Well, I think that's enough of that. Turn it off, I can't hear myself think. D'you know I often wish – I often wish my mother had forced me to learn the piano when I was young.

DUD. Yer, me too. If only she'd forced me to play, forced me to be a genius.

PETE. You wouldn't be here now, would you?

DUD. No, exactly.

PETE. You'd be in Vegas with some blonde girl.

DUD. Playing that Latin American boogie. But you know I remember when I was a nipper, I used to hate people who played the piano, like Enid Armstrong.

PETE. Oh Enid, she had a gift for the piano, didn't she?

DUD. Yer, she did, that was about all she had a gift for. I mean I used to go round to Goodmayes Park to play football, and I remember I used to see her playing in her window, and she used to pretend that she didn't know that everyone could see her through the curtains. She always used to have the window open even if it was freezing cold just so people could hear her playing 'The Rustle of Spring.' Showing off, y'know.

PETE. Mind you, Enid had a wonderful ear for music.

DUD. Yer, oh wonderful.

PETE. Her left one.

DUD. Left one, yer, the right one was completely useless.

PETE. A terrible ear, her right one.

DUD. Blocked up with wax.

PETE. She could have been a professional y'know, she was toying with the idea of becoming a professional.

DUD. Concert pianist . . .

PETE. . . . concert pianist at the Wigmore – er, Auditorium. And unfortunately her musical career, as you know, came to an end when she fell under the bus.

DUD. Yer.

PETE. She never played another note after that.

DUD. Never breathed another breath either, did she?

PETE. That's right actually, I remember now, she stopped breathing at the same time as she stopped playing the piano.

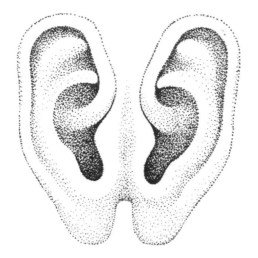

DUD. Died under the influence of bus.

PETE. But suffering can be a wonderful boon to the musician, you know. Take an example – Beethoven. Beethoven as you know was born in – er, Flanders, and er, it was a nice family y'know, fairly well to do. His mother was a weaver, and er, his father was a wearer.

DUD. Yer.

PETE. And Beethoven was a happy young child, you know. Did a little light composing in the lovely town of Bruges, where the tapestries caught on so well during the fourteenth century – you know hawks on the wrist and everything – and he wrote a few light-hearted tunes.

DUD. Jingles.

PETE. Jingles, basically, for the sales conferences of the tapestry-makers. He did one, what was it – er, 'Come and see our tapestry, No better one you'll see.' It wasn't y'know brilliant, competent but . . .

DUD. Not brushed with the stamp of genius.

PETE. But one day, as good fortune would have it, he suddenly became struck down with pleurisy, lumbago and athlete's foot.

DUD. And lightning.

PETE. . . . yer lightning . . .

DUD. 'Cause, there's always that picture of him shaking his fist at the thunderstorm.

PETE. And suddenly he was plunged into the most miserable state. He sank to the bottom and peered over the abyss of insanity. But he crawled back from the pit.

DUD. Over the hard rocks of endeavour . . .

PETE. . . . a new man. He saw what life was all about – misery and suffering, and suddenly this wonderful music began to pour out of his fingers, and he locked himself away and composed like a demon.

DUD. Yer, but, of course, while he did that, Pete, he forgot everything else. He forgot to feed himself, clean himself, his toilet habits went to pot, and the laundry used to come round every week, knock on the door, but they could never get any laundry out of Mr Beethoven. 'Mr Beethoven, Mr Beethoven, open up and let us have your laundry.'

PETE. Too busy composing. As soon as he'd worn out one lot of clothes he'd pull them off and shove on the next lot of clean ones.

DUD. Exactly. And the laundry used to pile up at the door, on the windows, shelves, and on the piano muffling all the strings so that he thought he was going deaf. He couldn't hear himself.

PETE. And the good people of Bruges outside, – they couldn't hear through all the piles of linen that wonderful Fifth Symphony.

DUD. Yer.

PETE. All they heard was a very muffled, 'Da-da-da-*dah*. . . .'

DUD. 'Da-da-da-*dah*.' 'I can't hear.' 'Da-da-da-*dah*.' 'What's the matter with my ears?' cried Ludwig.

PETE. And then eventually he passed away, and they found him –

DUD. Lying in a heap of manuscript and old baked-bean tins, and apricot slices . . .

PETE. And his underwear, 'cause when he ran out of paper Beethoven used his underwear in his frenzy of composing and all over his underwear is written his last symphonies. His string concerto on his Y-fronts and his organ concerto on his string vest.

DUD. Yer.

PETE. And all the underwear is preserved to this day – seventeen tons of it – in the Munich Museum of Beethoven's undies. A wonderful sight. The very stuff on which he composed. It would be wonderful, wouldn't it, to write a tune which would linger on for centuries.

DUD. Yer, and you'd know that when your bones have gone to clay and your dust had gone to something or other, whatever it is, that you'd written a tune like 'Robin's Return' and people would be whistling it.

PETE. I'd like to have done that 'Gypsy Flea' by Leroy Anderson.

DUD. Yer, wonderful.

PETE. Isn't it amazing how music can conjure up a whole era of the past which you'd forgotten about? Just a tune will suddenly bring back a whole scene.

DUD. Like when I cycled up Chadwell Heath to get some bananas for my mum. On the way back down Wood Lane, I could hear Mrs Woolley's gramophone blaring out Caruso singing 'Oh, for the wings of a

dove' and I was so carried away with it that I didn't see a small orange in the road and I fell off my bike and squashed my bananas. And every time I see squashed bananas, immediately it comes to mind – 'Oh, for the wings of a dove.'

PETE. Like with me whenever I hear Ravel's 'Bolero' I think of Eileen Latimer. I can't think why I keep thinking of her whenever I hear that tune. I think it may be due to the fact that she came round to tea one day and smashed the record over my head.

DUD. That could be the link.

PETE. Let's hear the other side of Debussy's Mother.

On Sex

PETE. Come over here, will you please.

DUD. Here, you've been ferretting around in my
sandwich box, haven't you?

PETE. I certainly have, and I found something not altogether connected with sandwiches. I refer of course to Blauberger's *Encyclopaedia of Sexual Knowledge*. How do you explain this?

DUD. I found it on the Heath, Pete, and I thought I better keep it in my sandwich tin to keep it dry until someone claimed it.

PETE. You're hiding it away, aren't you, because you're ashamed of it.

DUD. No I'm not. I just kept it there for safe keeping.

PETE. You shouldn't be ashamed of sex, Dud. It's no good hiding your sex away in a sandwich tin. Bring it out in the open.

DUD. It's a good book that, some good bits in it. Have you read any of it?

PETE. Yes, I've been through it up to page three thousand and one.

DUD. You've read the whole lot of it then, haven't you?

PETE. Yer, it's quite good.

DUD. I like it because it tells you everything about sex from the word go.

PETE. It's wonderfully informative about the sexual mores throughout the ages, Dud.

DUD. And it tells you of human sexual endeavour from the time of Adam and Eve, Pete.

PETE. It certainly does, all the myths about it as well. Of course, Adam and Eve while they were in the Garden of Eden, they didn't have anything to do with sex to start with, you know. When they were in Paradise, they didn't have anything to do with sex 'cause they were wandering around naked but they didn't know they were naked.

DUD. I bet they did know. I mean, you'd soon know once you got caught up on the brambles.

PETE. They had no idea – they were remarkably stupid,

as well as naked. They didn't know they were naked until up come a serpent – as some authorities have it. Up come a serpent and said, 'Here's an apple. Lay your teeth into that'. Then they laid their teeth into the apple and the serpent said, 'You're nude, you're completely nude.'

DUD. Hello nudies! Course they dashed off into the brush and covered themselves with embarrassment, didn't they?

PETE. And mulberry leaves as well. They covered themselves altogether with this primitive clothing made of leaves, and suddenly, as soon as they became completely covered, they began to get attracted to each other, and then, of course, they tore off the mulberry leaves and it all started, the whole business.

DUD. Well, I think once you've got clothes on you're more attractive to other people. Like I think Aunt Dolly's more attractive with her clothes on than off. So Uncle Bert says, anyway.

PETE. Well, Aunt Dolly is really at her most attractive when she's completely covered in wool and has a black veil over her face and, ideally, she should be in another room from you.

DUD. Who's your sort of ideal woman, Pete?

PETE. Well, above all others I covet the elfin beauty, the gazelle-slim elfin beauty, very slim, very slender, but all the same, still being endowed with a certain amount of . . .

DUD. Busty substances.

PETE. Yes, a kind of Audrey Hepburn with Anita Eckberg overtones is what I go for. What do you like?

DUD. Me? The same sort of thing. Actually I like the sort of woman who throws herself on you and tears your clothes off with rancid sensuality.

PETE. Yes, they're quite good, aren't they? I think you're referring to 'rampant sensuality'.

DUD. Either one will do. Of course, the important thing is that they tear your clothes off.

PETE. That's the chief thing. I like a good rampant woman.

DUD. I tell you a rampant woman – or rancid – or whatever you prefer. That's Veronica Pilbrow. Do you remember her?

PETE. Do I remember her? Yer.

DUD. She was always throwing herself on Roger Braintree, never me, though.

PETE. Well Roger Braintree at school, he always knew more than anyone else. He was always boasting about things he knew.

DUD. Old clever drawers, weren't he, eh?

PETE. You remember that time he came round behind the wooden buildings and he had, what was his name, Kenny Vare with him, and he come up and told me, 'I've discovered the most disgusting word in the world. It's so filthy that no one's allowed to see it except bishops and nobody knows what it means. It's the worst word in the world.'

DUD. What was the word?

PETE. He wouldn't tell me. I had to give him half a pound of peppermints before he let it out. Do you know what it was?

DUD. No.

PETE. 'Bastard.'

DUD. What's that mean Pete?

PETE. Well he wouldn't tell me. I knew it was filthy but I didn't know how to use it. So he said the only place I could see it was down at the Town Hall in the enormous dictionary they have there, – an enormous one with a whole volume to each letter. You can only get in with a medical certificate. So I went down there and sneaked in, you know, very secretively, and went up and took down from the shelf this enormous great dusty 'B' and opened it out and there was the word in all its horror – 'BASTARD'.

DUD. What was the definition, Pete?

PETE. It said, 'BASTARD – Child born out of wedlock.'

DUD. Urrgh! What's a wedlock, Pete?

PETE. A wedlock, Dud, is a horrible thing. It's a mixture of a steam engine and a padlock and some children are born out of them instead of through the normal channels and it's another one of the filthiest words in the world.

DUD. Make your hair drop out, if you say it. I like looking words up in the dictionary. You know, I like going round the Valence library and going to the reference library and getting out the dictionary of unconventional English and looking up 'BLOOMERS'.

PETE. Yer, it's quite a good way of spending an afternoon.

DUD. Course I tell you what, Pete, the whole business of sex is a bit of a let-down really when you compare it with the wonderful romantic tales of a novelist who can portray sexual endeavours in so much better form, Pete.

PETE. Well, he makes it all so perfect. In the hands of a skilled novelist, sex becomes something which can never be attained in real life. Have you read Nevil Shute?

DUD. Very little.

PETE. How much of Nevil Shute have you read?

DUD. Nothing.

PETE. Yes, well Nevil Shute is a master of sensuality. He has some wonderful erotic passages, like in *A*

Town Like Alice in the hardcover version, page 81. If you go down the library, it falls open at that page. It's a description set in Australia, Dud, and there's this ash-blonde girl, Tina.

DUD (*sings*). Tina, don't you be meaner . . .

PETE. Shut up. And she's there, standing on the runway, you see, of this aerodrome and it's very hot – Australian bush heat. It's very hot indeed and she's standing there waiting for her rugged Aussie pilot to come – bronzed Tim Bradley – and it's very hot. The cicadas are rubbing their legs together making that strange noise.

DUD (*essays cicada impression*).

PETE. Very similar to that nasty noise which is coming from your mouth at this very moment. And it's very hot and she's covered in dust. The Australian dust is all over her. She's got dust on her knees, dust on her shoulders . . .

DUD. Dust on her bust, Pete.

PETE. Dust on her bust, as you so rightly point out, Dud. And it's very dusty and it's very hot. Hot and dusty. And suddenly, out of nowhere, the clouds open.

DUD (*thunderclap impression*).

PETE. There's a tremendous clap of thunder and suddenly the mongoose is on her. The tropical rain storm is soaking through the frail poplin she is wearing and as the dress gets damper and damper, damper and damper, her wonderful frail form is outlined against the poplin. And then what does she hear but, in the distance, the distant buzzing of an approaching plane.

DUD (*plane impression*).

PETE. She cups her ear to hear, like this.

DUD. She cups her perfectly proportioned up-thrusting

ear, Pete.

PETE. She cups it; the plane comes down on the runway and comes to a halt and out comes the bronzed Aussie. But all the propellors are going very fast still. There's a tremendous rushing wind and it blows up against her and it blows the damp dress right up against her and reveals, for all the world to see, her perfectly defined . . .

DUD. Busty substances.

PETE. Busty substances.

DUD. What happened after that Pete?

PETE. Well, the bronzed pilot goes up to her and they walk away, and the chapter ends in three dots.

DUD. What do those three dots mean, Pete?

PETE. Well, in Shute's hands, three dots can mean anything.

DUD. How's your father, perhaps?

PETE. When Shute uses three dots it means, 'Use your own imagination. Conjure the scene up yourself.' Whenever I see three dots I feel all funny.

DUD. That's put me in the mood to go up to the Valence library and look up 'BOSOM' again.

PETE. No, it's no good looking up 'BOSOM', it only says '*see* BUST.'

DUD. But it's nice to read it all again.

PETE. It gives you something to do.

The Futility of Life

DUD *gives* PETE *a cup of tea.*

DUD. Tea's up, Pete.

PETE. No, thank you.

DUD. What, no tea?

PETE. Would you like me to submit a memo? No.

DUD. Oh. Have you got the collywobbles or something? You feeling a bit peaky?

PETE. No.

DUD. I thought perhaps those whelks might be clashing with the éclairs.

PETE. They are not, and if they were I would keep it to myself.

DUD. I'm not sure that you'd have the option. What's the matter?

PETE. No words can convey the merest inkling of my innermost feelings.

DUD. On the contrary. What you've just said has conveyed to me in detail the nature of your malaise. You're feeling a bit droopy.

PETE. A bit droopy? You're the sort of person who'd have gone up to Joan of Arc as the flames licked round her vitals and said, 'Feeling one degree under? Like a nice cup of tea?'

DUD. You know what my mother would say?

PETE. No.

DUD. 'Somebody has got out of bed the wrong side this morning.'

PETE. If your mother said that to me today, I'd smash her in the teeth with the coal scuttle.

DUD. Oh, I see. You're feeling a bit temperamental. As Dr Groarke would say – half temper, half mental . . . ha ha.

PETE. These glib platitudes are, if anything, exacerbating an already unbearable mood of depression.

DUD. If you're depressed, there's no point sitting around feeling sorry for yourself. That won't get the washing-up done.

PETE. Dud, your uncanny grasp of domestic trivia is of negligible therapeutic value, and if you tell me to pull myself together or snap out of it, I might well do something rash.

DUD. I wouldn't say anything like that. Get a grip on yourself, look on the bright side.

DUD *and* PETE (*together*). Count your blessings.

DUD. Ooh, Mr Acid Drop himself. Come on, you'll feel better if you get it off your chest. You can confide in me. I mean, what am I here for?

PETE. In your fumbling way you have actually articulated the fundamental question. What are you here for? What am I here for? What is the purpose of life?

DUD. The purpose of life? Well, we are here on this earth for a brief sojourn; life is a precious gift; the more we put into it, the more we get out of it; and if on the way I can have spread a little sunshine, then my living shall not be in vain.

PETE. Thank you, Patience Strong. Have you ever thought about death? Do you realise that we each must die?

DUD. Of course we must die, but not yet. It's only half past four of a Wednesday afternoon.

PETE. No-one knows when God in His Almighty Wisdom will choose to vouchsafe His precious gift of Death.

DUD. Granted. But chances are He won't be making a pounce at this time of day.

PETE. As far as I'm concerned, He can get a bloody move on.

DUD. That's morbid. Think of all the good things in life.

PETE. Like what?

DUD. Just look out the window.

He opens the curtains and closes them rapidly.

Perhaps not.

PETE. I think it was rightly said, 'See Dagenham Dye Works and die'.

DUD. Yes, but think of all the happy times you've had. That's what I do when I'm feeling below par. This room is filled with joyous memories. Look at this. A certificate proving we've been up the Post Office Tower.

PETE. And why did we go up it?

DUD. Because it was there, Pete, a challenge.

PETE. A brief escape from a life consisting of cups of tea, interminable games of Ludo and the occasional visit to your Aunt Dolly.

DUD. Well, what does this remind you of?
He shows PETE *a souvenir programme.*

PETE. It reminds me of our dismal visit to the Planetarium.

DUD. That was nice, wasn't it? Seeing the sky at night during broad daylight.

PETE. And emerging into a cold wind and drizzle, buying a newspaper only to read the headline 'London Airport Disaster – thirty old ladies sucked to death in Jumbo Jet engine.'

DUD. But think of the millions of old ladies who weren't sucked to death in a jet engine, who are now happily playing snap up and down the country.

PETE. The mental image of millions of old ladies shouting 'Snap' at each other merely confirms my ideas about the futility of life.

DUD. What about that time we went to the National Gallery then?

PETE. And you spent four hours with your nose up against one of Rubens's more voluptuous nudes.

DUD. I was bewitched by the Dutch master's handling of light and shade.

PETE. With particular reference to busty substances.

DUD. My apparent concentration on this area was due to the fact that I had heard that Rubens had used these busty appurtanences to obliterate an earlier more controversial study of Clapham Common.

PETE. Did you perceive any blades of grass peeping through the opulent pink orbs.

DUD. No, but I could see the dim outline of Battersea Power Station looming up through her nether regions. I think I've got the postcard somewhere.

PETE. Yes, it's up in the bedroom amongst your art collection of 'Spick and Span' and 'Beautiful Britons'.

DUD. Actually, I think you borrowed it to use as a book-mark for your copy of *La Vie Parisienne* . . . or was it *Lilliput*, edition number 159? One or other of your nudie books.

PETE. I purchased that copy of *La Vie Parisienne* for the very interesting article on marine life by Captain Cousteau.

DUD. Strange then that it should always fall open at a page not so much connected with the sea bed as with a scantily clad adagio dancer from the Moulin Rouge.

PETE. That must have been caused by the previous owner. I'm not interested in that sort of thing.

DUD. No wonder you're depressed. It's not healthy not to be interested in ladies of the opposite sex.

PETE. Well I'm not.

DUD. I don't believe you. Own up. Spring is here and perhaps disquieting emotions are seething beneath your mackintosh.

PETE. Nothing is seething beneath my mackintosh save for a general feeling of despair and futility and boredom with you.

DUD. I know. I know what will perk you up. 'Sausages and Mash'.

PETE. I'm not hungry.

DUD. No, the game, 'Sausages and Mash'. You read a book out loud and put the word 'sausage' for every word beginning with 's' and 'mash' for every word beginning with 'm'. It's very funny.

He gets a book.

Look what happens. 'I mash go down to the sausages again, to the lonely sausage and the sausage. And all I ask is a tall sausage and a sausage to sausage her by . . .' John Mash.

PETE. Bloody stupid.

DUD. Bloody sausage, you mean, – I mean you mash. I mash, you mash.

PETE. What's this then. 'Sausage sausages sausage sausages on the sausage sausage. The sausages sausage sausages are sausage sausages for sausage.'

DUD. Keats?

PETE. No, 'She sells sea shells on the sea shore.' We could also waste our time playing 'Fish and Chips.'

DUD. I don't know that one.

PETE. I'll give you an example. Why don't you fish off, chip chips.

DUD. I don't get that one. Fish off?

PETE. I'll give you a clue. The 'chips' in 'chip chips' stands for 'chops'.

DUD. Oh I see, so it's 'Why don't you fish off chip chops.' Oh, I sausage what you mash.

PETE. What?

DUD. I see what you mean.

At the Zoo

DUD. Nice and warm in here, isn't it, Pete?

PETE. Nothing like a nice warm reptile house.

DUD. Nothing like a nice warm reptile house.

PETE. Have you seen those geckos over there?

DUD. Geckos, what are they?

PETE. A gecko, Dud, is a lizard what has sucking pads
on its feet.

DUD. So it can hang on glass.

PETE. It can if it likes. It can hang on anything it fancies. It has a wonderful life, except, of course, it has to eat flies. Did you know that?

DUD. No I didn't.

PETE. Oh yes, it has to eat flies, 'cause, as you know, God created it, like he did everything else in his almighty wisdom, and all the animals have to eat each other to keep the population down. And geckos got lumbered with flies. It's all right when it's born. Its mother gives it some flies, all mashed up, daintily garnished with a daisy on top of it, so it can't tell what it's eating. But as soon as it learns to speak, Dud, and communicate, it says to its mother, 'Excuse me, what's this I'm eating?' and she has to reply 'Flies.'

DUD. 'Darling'.

PETE. Of course. She says, 'Flies, darling, and they're very good for you.' But that's why the gecko doesn't live very long, because he can't bear eating the stuff.

DUD. Eating flies, I couldn't bear that. I wouldn't like to be a gecko. I'd like to be a poisonous snake, – get a real feeling of power with all them fangs.

PETE. Well you've got prominent teeth already, haven't you?

DUD. I could sharpen 'em up and put a bit of cyanide in 'em and go round and, you know, sort of put my teeth into people's arms and kill 'em.

PETE. What sort of a poisonous snake would you be? Would you be an asp?

DUD. No I'd like to be a viper.

PETE. That's the same thing as an asp but an asp's bigger, Dud.

DUD. Is it?

PETE. Asp was a word invented by Shakespeare during the thirteenth century to denote a viper, 'cause, as you know, Shakespeare was a wonderful writer.

DUD. Knockout.

PETE. And he was doing this wonderful verse play about Cleopatra – how she got wrapped up in the carpet. Shakespeare had been writing this couplet to describe the scene when the snake comes rustling up her undies and begins to start biting into her busty substances. And he'd almost finished this magnificent verse couplet, you see, but the only thing is he only had one syllable left to describe the snake, and 'viper' was too long for the snake so he invented the word 'asp', and a very good word it is too.

DUD. Wonderful. I suppose it was a sort of Shakespearian abbreviation for 'A Stinging Personality'.

PETE. A.S.P., yes I suppose that's the reason.

DUD. Here, I don't reckon it was as asp what stung Cleopatra in the chest, I bet it was a bra constrictor.

PETE. What do you mean? It was an asp.

DUD. No, a bra constrictor, Pete – boa constrictor, it's a joke, Pete.

PETE. Oh, it was a joke, was it? Oh. It was very bad taste. You shouldn't make jokes about people who are dead, 'cause they can't fight back, Dud.

DUD. Sorry, Pete.

PETE. I wouldn't be a reptile at all if I had a choice. If I had a choice I'd be something lovely and cuddly and lovable. Something like those lovely humming birds, which hum with their various hues above the flowers. Those long tongues, all coiled up like watch springs. They can poke them out to forty yards long. A humming bird, Dud, can kiss at immense distances.

DUD. That means that you could stand on the Chiswick flyover and kiss someone up the Staines bypass.

PETE. Hovering four foot above the ground and humming, a wonderful opportunity. I tell you a creature I think is a very cuddly little thing, that's the chameleon. Very versatile.

DUD. Versatile creature, Pete. They can take on the shape and colour of anything they like, all the hues. You remember Mr Rigby?

PETE. Yer.

DUD. He nearly went through a wedding ceremony with one.

PETE. He would have been very happy with a chameleon. They make lovely wives.

DUD. You know, I was here last week, Pete, I don't know if I told you,

PETE. Yer.

DUD. I saw this big sign saying 'Topical fish this way'. I thought, that's OK, see a few topical fish, a few up-to-the-minute bits of satire. You know, topical barbs about the current situation in the world today.

PETE. What did you see?

DUD. Well I go in there and it's just a lot of fish swimming about, more timeless than topical.

PETE. I tell you what you done, you gone into the tropical fish department – that's *tropical* rather than topical, you see. What happens is that during the winter months, all through the blustery weather, sometimes some of the letters become dislodged because of the gales. And obviously the letter 'r' had become dislodged in this way. I was talking to the keeper about it actually, and he said that very often during the winter months, his 'r's blew off. During the winter months, his 'r's blew off.

DUD. I think I've had enough of the reptile house. Let's go on to the wonkey house.

PETE. No, that's an 'M' what's got blown upside down.

At the Art Gallery

DUD. Pete! Pete! Peter! Oh look, there you are.

PETE. I'm looking at 'The Passing-out of the Money Lenders'.

DUD. I don't care about that. I've been looking for you for the last half hour. We said we'd rendez-vous in front of the Flemish Masters.

PETE. No we didn't, Dud, we never said anything of the sort.

DUD. When I last saw you you were in the Breugel, weren't you?

PETE. That's right. I said I'd whip through the Abstracts, go through the El Greco, up the Van Dyke and I'd see you in front of the bloody Rubens.

DUD. I said I was going to go round the Velasquez, through the Abstracts, up the Impressionists and meet you in front of the Flemish Masters.

PETE. No you didn't, Dud. It doesn't matter anyway.

DUD. Here have a sandwich. My feet are killing me.

PETE. What's that got to do with the sandwich?

DUD. Nothing, I just said it afterwards, that's all.

PETE. Well you shouldn't say things like that together, it could confuse a stupid person.

DUD. Y'know, Pete, I reckon there's a lot of rubbish in this gallery here.

PETE. Not only rubbish, Dud, there's a lot of muck about. I've been looking all over the place for something good.

DUD. I've been looking for that lovely green gipsy lady, you know the one with –

PETE. The one with the lovely shiny skin.

DUD. Where is she? Nowhere.

PETE. Nowhere.

DUD. So I went up to the commissionaire. I said 'Here'. I got him by the lapel. I said 'Here . . .'

PETE. 'Here . . .'

DUD. I said, 'Here . . .'

PETE. You didn't spit sandwich at him, did you?

DUD. Sorry Pete. Sorry about that. I said, 'Where's that

bloody Chinese flying horse then?'

PETE. What did he say?

DUD. He said, 'Get out.' So I had to run up the Impressionists for half an hour and hide out. But what I can't understand frankly, Pete, is that there's not a Vernon Ward gallery in here.

PETE. There's not a duck in the building, there's no Peter Scott, there's no Vernon Ward. Not a duck to be seen.

DUD. Nothing. The marvellous thing about Vernon Ward is that of course he's been doing ducks all his life.

PETE. Well, he's done more ducks than you've had hot breakfasts, Dud. If he's done anything he's done ducks.

DUD. He's done ducks in all positions.

PETE. Yer.

DUD. Ducks in the morning, ducks in the evening, ducks in the summer time. What's that song?

DUD *and* PETE (*sing*). Ducks in the morning, Ducks in the evening, Ducks in the summertime . . .

DUD. Thought I recognized it.

PETE. The thing what makes you know that Vernon Ward is a good painter is if you look at his ducks, you see the eyes follow you round the room.

DUD. You noticed that?

PETE. Yer, when you see sixteen of his ducks, you see thirty-two little eyes following you round the room.

DUD. No, you only see sixteen because they're flying sideways and you can't see the other eye on the other side. He never does a frontal duck.

PETE. No, but you get the impression, Dud, that the other eye is craning round the beak to look at you, don't you? That's a sign of a good painting, Dud. If the eyes follow you round the room, it's a good

painting. If they don't, it isn't.

DUD. It's funny you say that, Pete, 'cause I was in the bathroom the other day –

PETE. Course you were, I remember that –

DUD. Course I was Pete, and I had the feeling of somebody in the room with me. I thought – funny – you know, and I didn't see no one come in and I thought – funny. And I felt these eyes burning in the back of my head.

PETE. Funny.

DUD. So I whip round like a flash and I see the bloody Laughing Cavalier up there, having a giggle. I felt embarrassed, you know.

PETE. Of course you would, Dud.

DUD. So I went out of the bathroom and I went to Mrs Connolly's across the road and asked if I could use her toilet.

PETE. Of course. You feel a bit daft with someone looking at the back of you.

DUD. She's all right, thought, 'cause she's only got a bowl of pansies in her toilet.

PETE. A real bowl of pansies or a painting, Dud?

DUD. A real painting.

PETE. Oh that's all right then. I tell you what's even worse, Dud, than the Laughing Cavalier.

DUD. What's that?

PETE. Can you think of anything worse?

DUD. No.

PETE. There is something worse than a Laughing Cavalier, what my Auntie Muriel has. She has the bloody Mona Lisa in her toilet.

DUD. That's dreadful.

PETE. That awful po-faced look about her, looking so superior, you know, peering down at you. She looks as if she'd never been to the lav in her life.

DUD. I mean that's the thing about the Laughing Cavalier, at least he has a giggle. He doesn't sit there all prissy.

PETE. No.

DUD. That's dreadful.

PETE. You been down the Rubens?

DUD. No.

PETE. You haven't seen the Rubens?

DUD. No.

PETE. There's one over there.

DUD. Is there?

PETE. Yer, he does all the fat ladies with nothing on. Great big fat ladies, naked except for a tiny little wisp of gauze that always lands on the appropriate place, if you know what I mean. Always the wind blows a little bit of gauze over you know where, Dud.

DUD. Course, it must be a million to one chance, Pete, that the gauze lands in the right place at the right time, you know.

PETE. Course it is.

DUD. I bet there's thousands of paintings that we're not allowed to see where the gauze hasn't landed in the right place – it's on their nose or something.

PETE. But I suppose if the gauze landed on the wrong place, Dud, – you know, landed on the nose or the elbow or somewhere unimportant, what Rubens did was put down his painting and go off to have lunch or something.

DUD. Or have a good look. Course you don't get gauze floating around in the air these days, do you?

PETE. No, not like in the Renaissance time. There was always gauze in the air in those days.

DUD. Course, similarly, you don't get those lovely little Botticelli cherubs.

PETE. They died out, of course – they hunted them down for their silken skin, you know.

DUD. No they didn't, they couldn't kill them, Pete, 'cause they were immortal.

PETE. No they weren't, they shot them through with arrows through their tiny little bellies and then their skin was turned into underwear for rich ladies and courtesans.

DUD. I reckon they went up to heaven like the angels.

PETE. No they didn't.

DUD. Course there's no call for angels now, is there?

PETE. No you don't see much of them these days, do you? Mrs Wisbey saw one actually the other day in the garden. She saw this angel. Actually it turned out to be a burglar. She went down on her knees praying to it and he was in the kitchen whipping away her silver.

DUD. Awful business.

PETE. Terrible. Have you seen that bloody Leonardo Da Vinci cartoon?

DUD. No.

PETE. I couldn't see the bloody joke. Went down there – nothing.

DUD. Well, of course, you know, Pete, people's sense of humour must have changed over the years.

PETE. Yes of course it has, that's why it's not funny any more.

DUD. I bet, when that Da Vinci cartoon first come out, I bet people were killing themselves. I bet old Da Vinci had an accident when he drew it.

PETE. Well, it's difficult to see the joke, just that lady sitting there with the children round her. It's not much of a joke as far as I'm concerned, Dud.

DUD. Well apart from that Pete, it's a different culture. It's Italian, you see.

PETE. It's Italianate.

DUD. We don't understand it. For instance, *The Mouse-trap* did terribly in Pakistan.

PETE. Another thing we've wasted public money on is that bloody Cézanne – 'Grandes Baigneuses'. Have you seen that load of rubbish?

DUD. No.

PETE. It's over there – there it is. Those fat, nude ladies with their bottoms towards you. That's 'Les Grandes Baigneuses'. You know what that means, don't you?

DUD. No what does it mean?

PETE. 'Big Bathers'.

DUD. Is that all?

PETE. That's all, 'Big Bathers'. £500,000 quid we paid for that. Those nude women come out of our pocket, Dud.

DUD. Well you could get the real nude ladies over here for that price. My Aunt Dolly would have done it for nothing.

PETE. She does anything for nothing, doesn't she? Dirty old cow.

DUD. And you can't tell whether it's a good painting or not, either, 'cause you can't see their eyes – whether they follow you round the room.

PETE. No, the sign of a good painting when its people's backs towards you is if the bottoms follow you round the room.

DUD. If it's a good painting the bottoms will follow you round the room?

PETE. Right.

DUD. Shall I test it, then?

PETE. They won't bloody budge, I'll tell you that much.

DUD. I can't look directly at the painting or else they'll know I'm looking and get all cagey.

PETE. Are they moving, Dud?

DUD. I think they're following me, Pete.

PETE. I don't think they are, Dud.

DUD. I reckon they are, Pete.

PETE. No those bottoms aren't following you around the room, your eyes are following the bottoms around the room.

DUD. The same thing, isn't it?

PETE. Course it isn't. There's a good deal of difference between being followed by a bottom and you following a bottom.

DUD. You come here, then, and see what I see.

PETE. I don't see anything at all – just a load of bottoms extremely stationary.

DUD. Well, you go that way and I'll go this way and you see if your bottoms move the same as mine.

PETE. That's difficult for the bottoms, if we go in different directions.

DUD. Well, they can divide up amongst themselves.

PETE. See what happens.

DUD. Mine are moving, Pete.

PETE. My bottoms haven't budged yet.

DUD. Mine are going beserk.

PETE. Mine haven't moved at all. You've got a fevered imagination. You coming?

DUD. No, I'll hang on a bit.

PETE. All right. See you in the Pissaro.

On the Bus

PETE. Right, Dud?

DUD. Right, Pete. Let's go and sit up the front, eh?

PETE. No, mustn't sit up the front, Dud, that's the least safe part of the bus. You ought to sit at the back, like you do in an aeroplane, that's when you're safe.

DUD. Why, what's wrong with the front?

PETE. Well, see, if there's a fatality, if the bus is involved in a fatal accident of any kind, it's the people up the front who get killed first, and the people up the back who get killed last.

DUD. Well, you get killed all the same though, don't you?

PETE. Yer, well you get killed about two seconds later, you see, and in those last two seconds of your life you might suddenly start to believe in God, or you'd be able to make out your will or something like that.

DUD. Oh I see, yer.

PETE. That's why I always sit at the back.

DUD. Yer. Course you know, I always look forward to these Saturday afternoon outings on a bus. I reckon these roustabout tickets are a real bargain.

PETE. The Red Rover roustabout ticket, it's fantastic value, Dud. For six and eight you have available six hundred and ninety-five thousand miles of British roadway. An unsurpassed view of the British countryside, and all the loveliness thereof. Course, the only trouble is you're not allowed off the bus.

DUD. Well it wouldn't be so bad if they had facilities on the bus.

PETE. Yer, as they don't have facilities most people have to get off after a couple of days. They can't stand it any longer.

DUD. You remember that clapped-out bus on the waste ground, behind the Green Lane Junior School?

PETE. Behind the wooden buildings?

DUD. That's right. Well, I thought, looks very nice, could make a little home out of that, and I went up there one night with a couple of blankets, and I went in and stayed there – it was a bit nippy, you know. I thought it's all right, but it's got no facilities.

PETE. Yer, so I suppose you had to nip off down the public. Well, they used to build facilities on the buses, you know, but all the people stayed on them, for years and years, they wouldn't get off 'em. In fact, my Auntie Muriel, she bought some second-hand facilities from the buses. She claims they're ex-army but they're not – you can see, 'London Bus Company' written all over them. Lovely work. I like to get on a bus because you meet a wonderful lot of people.

DUD. A wonderful class of people.

PETE. A wonderful opportunity to mingle with all types of people. Did I ever tell you about that tempestuous affair I had on the 82B.

DUD. They've stopped that route now, haven't they?

PETE. As a direct result of the incident I'm about to relate. I used to go on the 82B, as you know, and one day I got on it and sat down, in this seat here – well not this actual seat – but one in a similar position.

DUD. Course you did, Pete.

PETE. And I got on; the bell rang; I paid me fare; went on a couple of stops; the bus stopped; nobody got off and nobody got on. The bus went on; another stop; nobody got off; nobody got on. Went on another stop; nobody got off and nobody got on. Another stop; nobody got off; and nobody got on.

DUD. How long does this go on for, Pete?

PETE. It's a fairly uneventful journey, Dud, up to the crucial time – I'm trying to fill you in on the background. Suddenly we come to this stop under the overhanging elm what overhangs the road, just down by Farley Road. You know, it has a strange atmosphere about it.

DUD. Strangely romantic atmosphere about it, Pete.

PETE. Well anyway the bus drew to a halt, and onto the platform steps this uncannily beautiful woman with incredibly sensuous looks about her. She had sensuality written all over her face –

DUD. Did she really?

PETE. Well not literally, no – she just oozed sensuality –

DUD. I know – bit sweaty.

PETE. I sometimes wish, you know, that women would have 'sensuality' or something actually written over their face – 'sensuality' or 'frigidity'.

DUD. Yer – you'd know where you were then, wouldn't you?

PETE. You wouldn't waste your money.

DUD. What would you have if you had something written on your face, Pete?

PETE. I think I'd have 'dynamic lust' on my face.

DUD. I'd have 'insatiable passion'.

PETE. Anyway, this bird got on the platform, delicious looking girl, and I could see immediately what she was after.

DUD. Yer? What was she after, Pete?

PETE. Getting on the bus first of all, and secondly, she was filled with this crazy passion for me, you know. You could see it, she gave me this fleeting glance –

DUD. Like that, Pete?

PETE. Yer – very similar to the glance which you've just perpetrated, Dud. And she gave me this glance and immediately climbed upstairs. So I thought – funny, going upstairs, its obvious what she wants, me being downstairs and her going upstairs – funny. You can see what she's on. So I thought I'd play it very cool and stay downstairs. Sure enough, four stops later she comes down without even looking at me, got right off the bus and walked away.

DUD. What happened?

PETE. Well I stayed on – I thought I'm not going to give in to this sort of blatant blandishment, and I went on four stops and got off at Gribley Street, and I never saw her again.

DUD. You guessed her little game. Here, did I tell you about that bird, Joan Harold? About fourteen years ago.

PETE. Joan Harold. Spring of 1948.

DUD. That's right, right to the day.

PETE. Incredibly sensuous.

DUD. Yer, moist lips, loosely parted, flaring negroid nostrils.

PETE. Amazing gypsy laugh –

DUD. That's right. Anyway you know she used to get the five forty-five, 25B. Course she used to come out at five forty-five and I used to leave work about five, nowhere near where she was. So what I used to do, I used to get on a 62A up Chadwell Heath, then I used to get the 514 trolley down to the

Merry Fiddlers, then I used to have to run across that hill down by the railway bridge, over that field where the turnips were, over by the dye works, then I used to leap over the privet hedge, and hurl myself onto the 25B as it came round Hog Hill. There wasn't a bus stop there but it used to have to slow down because it was a very dangerous curve. I used to lie down in the middle of the road sometimes if it was going too fast. I used to leap on to the platform and spend about twenty minutes trying to get my breath back. Course I never spoke to her. Actually, once she got off and I got off in front and I said – 'Ere' – I thought I'd tease her a bit – coax her – and I said 'Chase me', and I started running off, but I was half way across Lymington Gardens before I realised she hadn't budged an inch.

PETE. That's no good Dud, play it cool. It's no good saying 'Chase me' and being that blatant, you got to play it extremely cool if you want to go out with women.

DUD. Well, I did go out with her once. I took her up West Ham speedway, and do you know, I gave her two cups of tea, a box of pontefract cakes and a ham sandwich – nothing.

PETE. Nothing?

DUD. Nothing.

PETE. How much did you spend on her?

DUD. About seven and three.

PETE. Seven and three and nothing? You must be a bloody fool. Its no good treating them like that, giving them pontefract cakes. I tell you what to do. Treat them extremely rough. You know I used to go up Gants Hill in 1953. Model aeroplane racing. Well I was standing down the bottom of Strawberry Lane –

DUD. What did you use to race?

PETE. I used to race a blue Spitfire. Elastic powered. I was waiting for the 91A which takes you to the top of Gants Hill –

DUD. They've discontinued that route now, haven't they?

PETE. Yer, due to the incident which I'm now about to relate. I was waiting by the stop with my Spitfire under my arm, and suddenly this fantastic bird come up to me, stood by me. She was an incredibly sensuous-looking creature with all the fire of Egypt plunging out of her peekaboo blouse, lightly covered with a see-through shirt –

DUD. And a teasing sweater.

PETE. She had a figure-hugging sweater on, and a duffle coat over the lot of it, and galoshes, and anyway she obviously delved deep into the works of Sartre –

DUD. Obviously spent a couple of years in view of the Seine with some randy poet.

PETE. She'd obviously done that sort of thing, and I could see immediately what she was after. It stands to reason – I'm standing by the bus stop, she comes up, stood to reason. She come to me and she was offering it on a plate –

DUD. Was she really?

PETE. Not literally, Dud, I sometimes wish they would. She said, 'Excuse me, does the 83B go up to Gants Hill'. You know what I said? I said, 'Maybe it does, maybe it doesn't, what business is it of yours, fat face'. That's the way to treat 'em, rough.

DUD. I don't know how you do it, Pete.

PETE. Oh it's quite easy, I just say the words.

DUD. What happened anyway?

PETE. I said, 'Get out of my life, I never wish to see you again, slatternly woman'.

DUD. What she do?

PETE. She took my advice – I never seen her again. That's the way – tell them what to do, they'll do it. If you say 'I never want to see you again', chances are you never will. Do you see those couple of birds up there? Which one do you fancy?

DUD. I fancy the one on the aisle.

PETE. The thin one? She could be yours tonight. In a matter of moments – if you play your cards right. Play it extremely cool. If I was you, Dud, if you fancy her – she's quite thin isn't she – go up to her and say something ironic and sophisticated, you know, like, 'Hello Fatty' – ironic. 'Hallo Fatty, come home with me and make love to me'.

DUD. Shall I do that then, Pete?

PETE. Yer. Go on up and see what happens.

DUD. All right.

He walks up the bus to the girl.

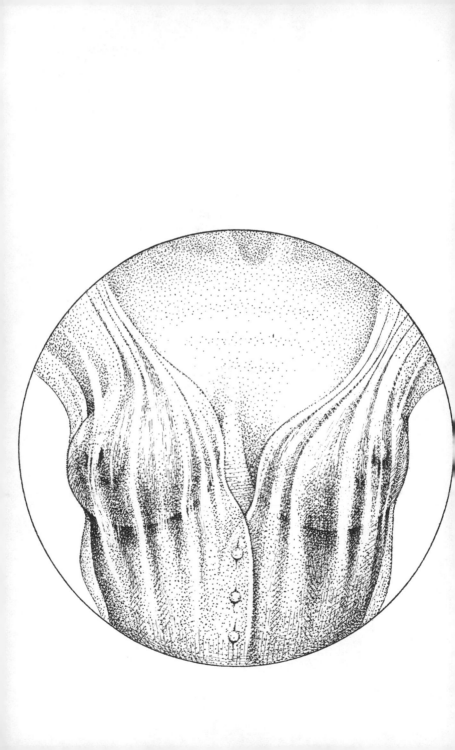

Hallo, fat face, come and make love to me tonight.

She slaps his face. DUD *goes back to his seat.*

PETE. What happened then?
DUD. Well I said, 'Hallo, fat face, come and make love to me tonight' and she slapped my face.
PETE. Yer. You see what she's wanting, don't you, stands to reason. You're well away.

By Appointment

PETE. Tea's up, Dud.

DUD. Nothing like a nice cup of tea, is there? Nothing like a nice cup of tea.

PETE. Nothing like it.

DUD. What's that you're reading, Pete?

PETE. Oh this is a wonderful book, Dud. It's steeped in history and everything else. It's *Burke's Peerages*.

DUD. *Burke's Peerages* – what's that?

PETE. It's a brilliant idea, it's a book which contains the names of the twenty thousand most noble people in the realm.

DUD. Who'd want to read that, Pete?

PETE. Well, the twenty thousand most noble people in the realm for a start. It's a superb idea, it all dates back to the eighteenth century, Dud, the Age of Reason. There was this Burke you see.

DUD. What was his name, Pete?

PETE. Burke, that was his name, one of the great Sussex Burkes – and he was wandering about his palatial parkland, you see, Dud, on a fine eighteenth-century summer morning, a lovely scene, as you can well imagine. The sun dappling through the trees.

DUD. His beautiful peacocks flaunting their exotic feathers in the sunlight.

PETE. Precisely, emitting a strange bird-like cry which sometimes comes from them. Suddenly it come to him.

DUD. What come to him, the peacock?

PETE. No, this wonderful concept come to him. He thought, 'Why don't I get hold of the names of the twenty thousand most noble people in the realm and flog it for two quid a time'. He made a fortune out of it.

DUD. Course he did. I could do exactly the same thing, couldn't I. I could go up Baron Road and knock on every door and say, 'Excuse me, Mrs Taylor, I wonder if you would give me your name and I'll put it in a book and flog it back to you'.

PETE. You'd do very well, the *Baron Road Gazette*.

DUD. Yer.

PETE. Could do very nicely with that sort of thing. Course the whole business of ancestry is extremely fascinating. I've been into my past, you know, I've traced myself back at Somerset House and do you know, in primordial times my great-great-great-grandfather come over with the Druids.

DUD. Oh, the Druids of Lymington Crescent.

PETE. George and Phoebe's ancestors.

DUD. I had a bit of bother, I went to Somerset House one morning – it was a nice morning, I thought, 'Go along to Somerset House, pop down look at the birth certificate – makes a change'. I went down there – I said to the gentleman behind the counter, 'Can I have a look at my birth certificate?' And so he got it out and I had a look and it said . . . it had my mother's name down there but where my father's name is supposed to be there was nothing there. I thought to myself 'Funny'. You know – mother's name here, father's name *not* here.

PETE. Funny . . .

DUD. Very peculiar. So I tackled my mother on this point but she was very evasive about it.

PETE. It was probably a foggy evening that magic night. But the wonderful thing about it, the ancestry business, is we've all got a bit of noble blood in our veins.

DUD. It's the best place for it isn't it?

PETE. Yes, it's a wonderful place for blood that.

DUD. Let's keep it that way.

PETE. Do you know that we're all in line for succession to the throne?

DUD. Really?

PETE. Well, if forty-eight million, two hundred thousand, seven hundred and one people died I'd be Queen.

DUD. Where would I come in that, Pete?

PETE. I think three quarters of the world has to pass away before you get there.

DUD. But what would you do if you were Queen, Pete?

PETE. I'd turn the job down, I wouldn't do it, too much like hard work.

DUD. I'd rather like to be Queen. I tell you what I'd do. I'd give the M.B.E. to Mrs Woolley and I'd give Aunt Dolly the Order of the Garter for services rendered to humanity.

PETE. Your Aunt Dolly could do with a bit of decoration, couldn't she?

DUD. Why wouldn't you like to be Queen, Pete?

PETE. The trouble is, you see, you're always being looked at. Wherever you go you're in the public eye. You go to the theatre, nobody looks at the stage, they're all looking at you. And it's like living in a goldfish bowl, Dud.

DUD. Well, I wouldn't mind living in that goldfish bowl Pete, I mean, that palace is at least twice the size of Dagenham Dye Works.

PETE. It's a nice area too. It's very handy for the West End.

DUD. West End, they don't need the West End. They got their own shops in there, their own cinema. I mean, it's the only place in the West End where they don't play the National Anthem after the film.

PETE. That's an advantage isn't it? Mind you, think of all the extra-mural expenses they have, the upkeep of the children, the clothing, the food for the pets.

DUD. I mean those royal corgis eat like horses.

PETE. Not to mention the royal seals all jumping up and down in the fountains. The money for their food has to come out of her pocket, you know. I mean it's a very busy life, you know. You only have to look at the royal diary to realize what a busy life it is.

DUD. Have a peep in the diary, boy, you get the message.

PETE. Yer, you get an indication, Dud. Seven thirty: got up. Cup of tea. Got into long car, waved, opened Parliament.

DUD. Got back, had lunch with Mr Wilson, got into long car, waved, cut ribbon, launched oil tanker.

PETE. Got back, Mr Wilson still there, looking round for his briefcase containing secret measurements of C. P. Snow, posed for Battle of Britain stamp, had tea with three thousand people, tried to meet them all.

DUD. Five o'clock, soaked right hand in methylated spirits. Six o'clock: practiced sitting on horse sideways. Seven o'clock: got into long car, waved, went to Commonwealth Dance Festival.

PETE. Eleven thirty: come home, cup of cocoa. Goodnight diary.

DUD. Terrible, isn't it?

PETE. Very, very busy life.

DUD. Very busy life that, Pete. Mr Wilson seems to hang about a bit doesn't he?

PETE. Well, he's always creeping round there, Dud. Course, being a socialist he's fascinated by all the trappings of royalty. Before becoming Prime Minister the grandest building he ever seen was the Hampstead Golf Club. He's always sniffing round there, fingering the gold lamé curtains.

DUD. Casting covetous eyes on the tapestries. On the other hand Her Majesty has the chance to meet some interesting people.

PETE. The trouble is, you see, although they're very interesting, when they get round the Palace they're so nervous they become boring. They're overawed by the occasion. Now the other day, Albert Einstein, the bloke who invented gravity, went round to collect his OBE.

DUD. His what?

PETE. His OBE for inventing the gravity. A very interesting person and a fine mind. The Queen was looking forward to meeting him, asking him a few questions, you see. So Einstein was waiting there, all tense, waiting for his medal. Her Majesty come up and stuck one on him and said to him 'Hello, Mr Einstein, how does all this gravity business work?' And Einstein was so nervous his teeth dropped out on the foor. Mind you, Her Majesty passed it off very nicely and said 'Aha, Mr Einstein, I see gravity is at work today', and with a tinkling laugh moved on to Tony Curtis who was picking up a baronetcy.

DUD. That's marvellous.

PETE. A wonderful thing to do.

DUD. What's the time, by the way?

PETE. It's about quarter past nine, Dud, and do you know, at this very moment, Her Majesty is probably exercising the royal prerogative.

DUD. What's that then, Pete?

PETE. Don't you know the royal prerogative? It's a wonderful animal, Dud. It's a legendary beast, half bird, half fish, half unicorn, and it's being exercised at this very moment. Do you know that legend has it that e'er so long as the royal prerogative lives, happiness and laughter will reign throughout this green and pleasant land.

DUD. And the yeoman will stand tall upon this sceptred isle, Pete.

PETE. The Archers will look out o'er the dales and see happy laughing children. Flaxen-haired Anglo-

Saxon youths will scan the foam-flecked waves for marauderers.

DUD *and* PETE (*sing*): Rule Britannia, Britannia rule the waves . . .

PETE. Course it does, Dud.

DUD. Course it does, Pete.

As Nature Intended

PETE. What are you doing?

DUD. I was just looking for a sixpence I dropped.

PETE. Why are you waving your legs in the air like a stag beetle on its back?

DUD. I thought the sixpence might have slipped under my bottom, but as it wasn't there I thought it might have trickled into my turn-ups – hence the vigorous shaking motions.

PETE. It looks to me as if you are trying to eliminate unsightly stomach sag.

DUD. I was combining the two operations – sixpence-searching and stomach-sag stiffening.

PETE. You seem to have an almost unhealthy obsession with your health since your visit to Doctor Groarke. What did he diagnose?

DUD (*exercising with a bullworker*). He said that I was in quite good condition for a man in my condition. There was a slight tendency to what he called 'executive bulge'.

PETE. 'Executive bulge' – due doubtless to your diet of caviar and crêpe suzette. More like sandwich spread if you ask me.

DUD. He suggested that I would do well to shed a few pounds here and there.

PETE. A fat lot he knows about dieting. He's all of eighteen stone in his stockinged feet.

DUD. Dr Groarke has glands and it's a personal tragedy. He eats like a sparrow.

PETE. You also go to a barber who is totally bald and rubs useless unguents into your scalp.

DUD. Lager and lime is very beneficial to the follicles, and hair, after all, is a man's crowning glory.

PETE. It's his crowning glory, is it? You rather hide your light under a bushel with that old cap of yours.

DUD. Speak for yourself.

PETE. Shall I switch the oven on so you can give it a blow wave? And a blue rinse might be a glamorous addendum to your beautiful coiffure.

DUD. There is nothing unmanly in taking pride in one's physical appearance. In Renaissance days men wore rouge, beauty spots, wigs, bras – all that sort of thing.

PETE. I see you fancy yourself as the new Adrian Street.

DUD. Who's he?

PETE. Adrian Street is the blond wrestler who, like you, seems to revel in the glories of his own physique.

DUD. Oh yer, a fine figure of a man. I love watching his superb Boston crabs and the way he sweeps back his hair after extricating himself from a triple knee-lock. Then he flexes his pectorals.

PETE. Whilst cracking walnuts with the other parts of his body.

DUD. I love the way he struts round the ring, taunting the crowd and flinging his golden mane all over the place.

PETE. Do you? I suppose you fancy yourself as a wrestler?

DUD. It would be a challenge.

PETE. And now, ladies and gentlemen, a catchweight contest over half a round. In the left corner Mick McManus, Les Kellet and Black Kwango and in the right-hand corner, wearing the pink lurex, Dud, the Dagenham dervish.

DUD. You've got to have a gimmick.

PETE. I should rely on your costume rather than your technique. Call yourself Dud, the man in the iron mackintosh.

DUD. I see myself more as a mad monk who prays for his victims between rounds but strangles them unmercifully with his rosary.

PETE. I doubt if you'd have the strength to climb into the ring let alone strangle anybody.

DUD. I think you underestimate my strength. Do not judge a sausage by its skin. Have you ever tried Indian wrestling?

PETE. No I've never tried Indian wrestling. What's that?

DUD. Indian wrestling. You put your hand up.

PETE. You put your hand up where?

DUD. And then I try to force it down.

PETE. And the winner is elected leader of the tribe.

DUD. Yer, come on, have a wrestle.

They lock hands.

PETE. I seem to detect in this childish struggle a strong underlying whiff of latent homosexuality.

DUD. Nonsense. What's homosexual about two grown

men sitting down and holding hands? Oh.

He unlocks rapidly.

PETE. Come on, aren't you enjoying it?

DUD. No. I think after all that exercise a nourishing snack is called for. It's half-time.

PETE. Ladies and gentlemen, no contest. Yes, make some tea and get out the rest of the Swiss roll.

DUD. If you wish to poison your body, Pete, on your own head be it. The tannin in tea is a dangerous and deleterious stimulant and furthermore it is addicting.

PETE. I may have had tea since I was a tiny but I could give it up like that.

DUD. That's what they all say. They start off on soft drinks, move on to tea for even bigger kicks and then it's downhill all the way to black espresso coffee, frothy cappucino and a lingering death surrounded by damp tea-bags.

PETE. What do you propose to substitute?

DUD. A glass of Adam's ale: water from the springs of Malvern – natural free-range spa water uncontaminated by chemical impurities.

PETE. At six bob a bottle.

DUD. A small price to pay for a prolonged active life.

PETE. What's all this rubbish you're preparing over here?

DUD. Natural, free-range fruit and vegetables, a nut salad with a smattering of brown rice to get my yin and yang balanced.

PETE. Did you get all this stuff from the health store?

DUD. Yer. Mr Jones supplies the only unpolluted produce in Dagenham.

PETE. I saw him getting his supply of free-range whisky from the Royal Oak last Sunday.

DUD. He doesn't drink: it was probably for a friend.

PETE. Doubtless he thought the safest way to convey the whisky to his friend was to carry it in his stomach; then to demonstrate his health and well-being he sang one bar of 'Nellie Dean', burped and fell effortlessly to the floor.

DUD. Mr Jones is not in the habit of taking unhealthy alcoholic bevies. It must have been his double.

PETE. Yes, he had several doubles and trebles.

DUD. Could you give me my wild thyme, please?

PETE. After that Indian wrestling I have a nasty feeling I could.

DUD (*switches on a sunray lamp over some cress*). This cress is coming on nicely.

PETE. Don't you think it a little unnatural to force it out of the flannel with a sunray lamp?

DUD. It is a compromise between nature and necessity. As you know, the one placed outside the window just collected a lot of soot and pigeon doodahs.

PETE. Very nourishing indeed. I'm looking forward to some nicely tanned cress.

DUD (*mixing a salad*). There we are: carrots, cauliflower, dates, nuts – remember not to bolt your nuts, Pete, ha ha – wild rice and, to cap it all, some invigorating honey.

PETE. Straight from your comb.

DUD. Get your teeth round this and you'll never yearn for a Swiss roll again.

PETE. It's quite tasty in a very dull kind of way. I see they've included a free-range grasshopper in the cauliflower.

DUD. It's good, though isn't it?

PETE. What are you twitching for?

DUD. It's not twitching. I'm doing isometric exercises. Keeps the facial muscles in trim, banishes crows' feet.

PETE. You dreadful old Narcissus. It's the sort of behaviour that would get you arrested in the underground.

DUD *jumps up and down on his chair.*

PETE. The stairs are outside the door, Mr Body Beautiful.

DUD. Oh blimey, I feel a bit dizzy.

PETE. I should sit down then. It's probably withdrawal symptoms.

DUD. What do you mean?

PETE. Well, you haven't had a cup of tea for eight hours; and, as you say, it is addicting, you can't just kick the habit like that. I'll get you a small medicinal dosage to get you on your feet again.

DUD. Thank you. And if there's any of that free-range Swiss roll about, I'd better force some of that down me.

PETE. And then if you're feeling up to it, why don't you combine this with Marine Exercise four hundred and eighty-one? Do you know what that is?

DUD. No.

PETE. Take the Swiss roll in your left hand and raise it rhythmically to the lips in time with the music.

He puts 'Wheels Cha Cha Cha' record on.

And one, two, three: up to the lips. Down two, three. Let the body do the work . . .

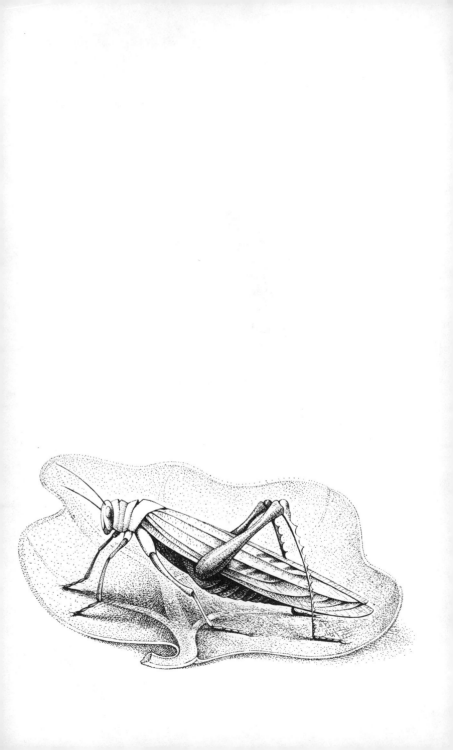

Worst Things

PETE. Hello Dud.

DUD. Hello Pete.

PETE. How are you?

DUD. Not so bad. Thought you might like a nightcap before we went to bed.

PETE. Yer. A nice cup of something or other never does you any harm.

DUD. Quite right there, Pete.

PETE. You know I've been thinking, Dud.

DUD. What you been thinking, Pete?

PETE. I was wondering what you thought was the worst thing that could possibly happen to you in all the world.

DUD. Oh – I don't know. What do you think is the worst thing.

PETE. What do you dread more than anything else? What would you find most horrible?

DUD. What would I hate happening to me more than anything else in the world?

PETE. Have you ever thought of that?

DUD. No I haven't.

PETE. I have. You know what the worst thing I can think of is?

DUD. What?

PETE. I'm in bed late one night, and I'm sort of drowsing and there's a wind howling outside, and suddenly –

DUD *does wind type noises.*

Yer, like that. Suddenly tap, tap, tap on the bloody door.

DUD. What's that?

PETE. I get up, I say, 'Who's there? Who's there?'

Nobody answers. Tap, tap, tap again. I go to the bloody door, and do you know what's there?

DUD. What?

PETE. Fourteen Nazi officers, with blond hair, great strapping louts, and they say, 'Ha ha, Herr Pete, ha ha, we've come to get you.' And they seize hold of me and they cram me into a cardboard box which is full of man-eating ants what haven't eaten for three months. They're bloody ravenous the ants. And they start eating me. Munch, munch, very slowly, till they've eaten me to death. That's the worst thing I can think of.

DUD. That's terrible, Pete.

PETE. What's the worst thing you can think of?

DUD. The worst thing I can think of is – er – I'm feeling a bit peckish and I go down to the kitchen to get a slice of Spam, and I turn the light on – there's no light. Light doesn't work.

PETE. Bulb doesn't work?

DUD. I think – funny, I put a new bulb in this morning, went very quickly. Funny. And then suddenly, I see this eerie glow in the corner of the kitchen, and there's something there. I say, 'Who's there?' and this voice says, 'It's me, the High Executioner. I've come to chop your head off.' And suddenly there's a great flare of light in the kitchen, and I see this bloke standing there, stripped to the waist, with a mask on. He's got a whacking great axe and he says, 'All right, Dud, this is it. Put your head over the basin and I'll chop it off.' And I scream and that. And he brings his axe down on me like that.

PETE. And that's the worst thing you can think of?

DUD. Yer.

PETE. Why that's nothing, mate, it's absolutely bloody

nothing compared to my ants, gnawing their way into my body and forty-eight Nazis outside with blond hair. It's bloody nothing!

DUD. Well, the thing is he only nicks me the first time, he just nicks my neck like that,

PETE. Oh, that's better, then.

DUD. And then he does it again and chops my head off, severs it. You know.

PETE. I still don't think it's as bad as my ants, you see, because the thing about my ants, what makes it even worse, is that they're strictly trained by the Nazis to eat very slowly. And what's more they've got a coagulant on their teeth,

DUD. What's that?

PETE. Coagulant? That's to stop you bleeding, you see, so that when they bite you they'll just eat the flesh away but you don't bleed. So it takes a long time and they eat you till there's nothing left of you but you're still alive and hurting and dreadful. That's pretty dreadful isn't it?

DUD. I tell you what I think would be dreadful, actually, Pete, is I go out in the garden because I've left a couple of pair of socks out there, and I don't want them to get frozen overnight, so I go out, and I start taking the socks down. I suddenly see, it's a very dark night you know, it's at night, and the moon's up and there's a cloud going across it, and I hear a wolf crying – (*He does a wolf noise*) – and I see this shape by the clothes pole,

PETE. What is it?

DUD. It's a lady, a woman, dressed in a tight black dress, slit up to here, and you can see her legs all sort of alabaster, glistening in the moonlight, and her eyes are cold like death. She's got these wolf fangs.

PETE. She's a wolf-woman is she?

DUD. She's a wolf-woman, and she says, 'Come here, Dud.' She beckons me with a sinuous hand.

PETE. She's got you mesmerised.

DUD. Yer, she's got me transfixed and she says, 'Come here, Dud, I've got something for you mate.' So I go down there and just as I get up to her she raises her hand and hits me round the face. And then vanishes like that.

PETE. And that's bad?

DUD. That's terrible.

PETE. That's bloody nothing mate. Being hit round the face by a wolf-woman. That happens every other day of the week. What are you worrying about there? I'll tell you a really bad thing. I'm staying down in the country. Staying with Daphne du Maurier, in her haunted house. And I just got to bed, I've been up the creaking stairs, creak, creak, creak, up the creaky stairs, the wind is howling through the tenements, or the battlements, or whatever they are. I get into bed, and I drowse off into a fitful doze. Suddenly I'm awakened by the cry of a single cock.

DUD *does crowing noise.*

Yer, much the same as that but much worse.

DUD. What time is it?

PETE. It's one o'clock.

They do chiming noises.

And I look up and there at the window is something amazingly horrible. It's a great white flabby substance, coming all over the window, covering it up. And I get up to go 'cause I'm scared of the nameless dread of it all. I start to rise and I find that I'm buckled down by gossamer threads.

DUD. You're chained to the bed?

PETE. I'm chained to the bloody bedpost by these gossamer threads.

DUD. What you wearing, Pete?

PETE. I'm wearing my red nightie.

DUD. The one with the roses round the lapel?

PETE. That's right. I'm chained down with the gossamer threads – I can't move. And then it's coming through the window.

DUD. What, the thing?

PETE. The thing. You know what it is? It's a giant man-eating slug. Of a type rarely found. And it comes in through the window, sliming and slurping, very inexorable.

DUD. What sort of noise does it make?

PETE. The slug?

DUD. Does it go sort of growl, growl?

PETE. No that's a bloody tiger going growl, growl. A slug, a man-eating slug of a type rarely found, that's coming through my window, goes sort of slurp, slurp, glug, glug.

DUD. It's horrible.

PETE. I hear the slug coming inexorably towards me, sliming all over the floor, and up over the end of the bed, up over the eiderdown, up over my body. And it says to me –

DUD. It talks, does it?

PETE. Yes, it talks, the slug. It says to me, 'All right Pete, this is it. I'm a slug and I've come to eat your bloody blood, mate.' And it puts its teeth into my neck – it's got teeth under its sluggish body,

DUD. Where's it got its teeth?

PETE. Under its neck. And it starts to suck the blood away and I faint into a dreadful coma. And I feel the blood leaving my body and get up into the slug, and I know it's all over.

DUD. That's awful.

PETE. That's a bloody sight worse than seeing a bloody old wolf-woman in the garden, I'll tell you that much. Having this slug come up through your window.

DUD. I hadn't thought of that one.

PETE. No.

DUD. Well, shall we go to bed? I wouldn't mind actually kipping down here tonight. It's a bit creepy up there.

PETE. I'll go and get some more cocoa, shall I Dud?

DUD. All right. Would you, Pete?

PETE *goes off.*

Pete. Pete. Where you gone, Pete?

PETE (*whispers*). Tap, tap, tap.

DUD. Now, stop mucking about. Pete. Pete.

PETE (*whispers*). I am a slug. I've come to get you, Dud.

DUD. Oh stop it, Pete.

PETE. Creeping round the door to come and get you.

DUD. Turn the light on.

PETE. I am a giant man-eating slug, slurp, slurp.

DUD. Turn the light on Peter, turn the light on.

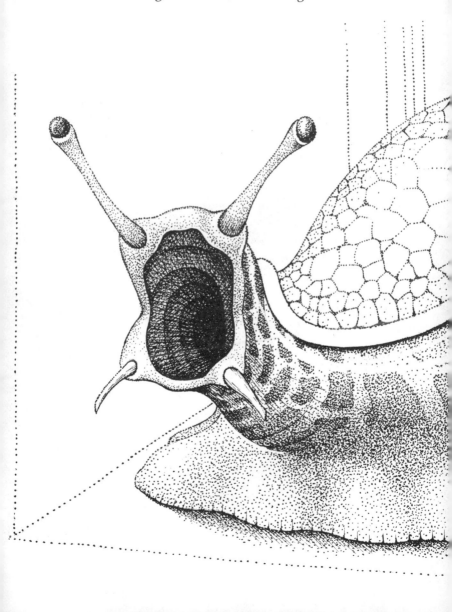

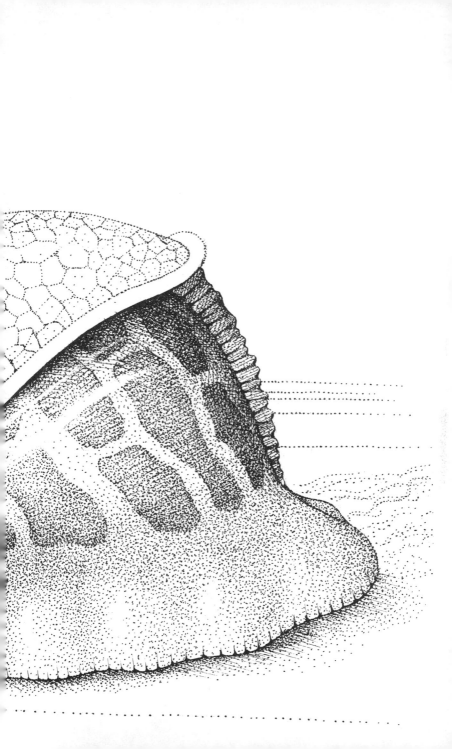

The Wardrobe

DUD *gets out of bed, sleepwalks, returns to bed and wakes up with a scream.*

DUD. Where am I?

PETE. You're in bed.

DUD. Who are you?

PETE. I am me and you are Dud. You've just been sleep-walking again.

DUD. I've just had the most extraordinary dream. I keep getting it every night in colour.

PETE. Lucky old you.

DUD. It's a nightmare. It always starts the same way. I'm feeling very cold and then suddenly I'm walking down this endless corridor, opening door after door.

PETE. Just one moment, I'll jot this down.

DUD. Finally, I come to a staircase.

PETE. Oh dear.

DUD. And there's this lady at the top.

PETE. Scantily clad?

DUD. No, discreet twin-set and pearls – and it's always Mrs McDermott.

PETE. That friend of your mother's?

DUD. Yer, and she's beckoning me with her finger.

PETE. Good way to beckon.

DUD. So I go up the stairs and she vanishes and I find myself in this room, confronted by a wardrobe . . . just like this one.

PETE. Mahogany wardrobe confrontation.

DUD. And I've got this terrible urge to get inside it and yet I have this dread of being trapped inside and as I stand there the wardrobe starts to get bigger.

PETE. It's not you getting smaller?

DUD. Could be a bit of both.

PETE. Either or.

DUD. Anyway, it seems to get bigger and bigger and then when it's just about to overwhelm me I wake up in a cold sweat.

PETE. Going 'Aaaaaaahhhhh.'

DUD. What does it all mean?

PETE. Well, this is a very simple dream to interpret. I don't know whether you're familiar with the works of Freud.

DUD. I do have a cursory knowledge of his theories. I recently skimmed through his lectures to the students of Heidelberg on the phallic implications of the penis.

PETE. An interesting, if superficial study. Did you read it in the original German?

DUD. No, I read it in précis form on the back of a box of Swan Vestas.

PETE. I'm afraid it loses a lot in translation. Freud's basic theory – to which in general I adhere – is that every human action, conscious or unconscious, is motivated by the sex drive.

DUD. Ah, the sex drive. You mean when you get girls in the back of the car and drive up the M1 and bung 'em one.

PETE. The serious German doctor was not referring to sexual shenanigans in the back of a Volkswagen.

DUD. Sorry, Pete.

PETE. He maintains that sex is behind everything we do.

DUD. You mean everything we do is based on sex? What about reading a newspaper?

PETE. Exactly, the opening of a newspaper in Freudian terms is a symbolic rape.

DUD. I gave the *Radio Times* a right going over this evening then.

PETE. Shall we preserve a serious tone? Freud says you have your conscious mind and your subconscious mind – in your case the division is marginal. When you go to sleep your subsconscious takes over from your conscious and releases your hidden fantasies and desires – the inner you.

DUD. Does that mean that because I feel cold in my dream, deep down I'm frigid?

PETE. No, you were probably just feeling cold in bed and this became part of your dream. Fact can trigger off fantasy.

DUD. And, vice versa, fantasy can trigger off fact.

PETE. I don't catch your gist.

DUD. Like when a dream comes true. You dream you're going along to the bathroom and then you wake up and find that you haven't been to the bathroom . . . except that you have in a manner of speaking. Not that it's ever happened to me, but a friend told me about it.

PETE. He was incontinent.

DUD. No, it happened right here in England.

PETE. I would prefer not to dwell on your friend's nocturnal mishaps.

DUD. Exactly his feelings, Pete. He spent the rest of the

night drying off on the radiator.

PETE. In your dream you're going through a number of doors. Now, as any fool knows, doors represent years in your life.

DUD. I didn't know that.

PETE. As *most* fools know, a door represents a year in your life, so you are subconsciously returning to your childhood.

DUD. I then come to the staircase.

PETE. An obvious phallic symbol.

DUD. Mrs McDermott is standing at the top of it.

PETE. You climb up the staircase.

DUD. Up my phallic symbol.

PETE. And Mrs McDermott vanishes.

DUD. I don't blame her.

PETE. Then you're alone in a room with a menacing wardrobe. Now what do you think the wardrobe represents?

DUD. Er . . . a wardrobe?

PETE. Good guess. No, the wardrobe represents your mother and your desire to get into it shows an infantile yearning to return to the warmth and security of your mother's womb.

DUD. You're wrong there, Pete. I have absolutely no inclination to get back into the confines of my mother's womb.

PETE. Not consciously. I'm not suggesting that you go round to 439 Beacontree Avenue and ask your mum for readmission – it's three o'clock in the morning and anyway it's illegal. But I think that something traumatic occurred when you were being born that causes this yearning.

DUD. A yearning mingled with dread.

PETE. What happened that rainy night in Ward 10 in the Charing Cross Hospital that so profoundly scarred your psyche?

DUD. I don't know, I can't remember being born.

PETE. But your subconscious does. Now the only way we can free your subconscious, with its obsession with the womb, is to recreate symbolically the circumstances of your birth.

DUD. And through self-knowledge emerge a wholer man, a more whole man – feel better.

PETE. The wardrobe is your mother.

DUD. It's nothing like her.

PETE. But in your unconscious dream state it stands for your mother. I want you to imagine that this old brown mahogany wardrobe is your mother.

DUD. That's a bit tricky. But I suppose those two knobs at the top ring a bell and those huge creaky drawers are reminiscent.

PETE. Let's get you conceived. Be upstanding, please. It's nine months before you are born. You are nothing.

DUD. Not even anything?

PETE. Put it this way: you're a tiny little microscopic cell eager to meet up with your cell-mate. It's Saturday night. Fulham have won the Cup. Your Dad's been at the Green Chartreuse. Suddenly, the miracle of life occurs. Kindly enter your mother's womb.

DUD *enters the wardrobe.* PETE *slams the doors.*

PETE. You are now in your mother's womb, how does it feel?

DUD. Dreadful. Full of old socks and mackintoshes.

PETE. There are nine months to go before you are born. We won't take that literally otherwise we'll be here all night. Nine months to lift-out. Beginning count-down: zero minus eight, Dud, looking good.

DUD. Feeling dreadful, Pete.

PETE. Zero minus seven, zero minus six.

DUD. Arms and legs forming, Pete.

PETE. Zero minus five, zero minus four: heart and pulse satisfactory.

DUD. Zero minus three: beginning to kick about a bit.

DUD kicks at the doors.

PETE. Zero minus two.

DUD. Facial characteristics forming.

PETE. God help us! Zero minus one.

DUD. I like it here.

PETE. Zero. We have lift-out . . .

DUD. I don't want to. It's nice and warm here.

PETE. Zero plus one. Come out.

DUD. The door's jammed, Pete.

PETE. Come out, you little sod, you're a month overdue.

DUD pushes the doors open.

DUD. That's it, that's what the doctor said: 'Come out, you little sod, you're a month overdue.' No wonder I wanted to get back in.

PETE hits him on the bum with a cricket-bat.

What did you do that for?

PETE. To get you breathing, of course. You can thank your lucky stars you're not Jewish.

DUD. Does this mean that I won't ever have that dream again?

PETE. No danger, Dud: you are cured of your recurrent nightmare cycle.

DUD. That's marvellous, now perhaps I can get back to dreaming about Debra Paget.

They both get into bed.

PETE. Oh, the sheets have got chilly, I think I'll put a pullover on.

He goes to the wardrobe.

DUD. Here, leave my mother alone. Stop tampering with her drawers.

PETE. It's not your mother, it's a wardrobe.

DUD. Are you telling me I can't recognize my own
     mother? You never liked her, did you?
PETE. Not particularly. I think she could do with a boot
     up her side-panels.
DUD. Leave her alone. She's eighty-four and very frail.
     It's all right, Mum, don't worry. I'll look after you.

Religions

PETE. I was reading the Bible the other day, you know.

DUD. It's good, isn't it?

PETE. It's a very good book, Dud, it's beautifully done, it's beautifully bound, it's beautifully put together. I was reading that chapter about Ishmail begat Remus and Remus begat Isobar and Isobar begat this other bloke.

DUD. They were certainly begetting.

PETE. Yer. Every one begat each other.

DUD. Sort of, sort of historical document thing.

PETE. Like, you know, who gave birth to who and that.

DUD. Like at Somerset House, isn't it?

PETE. George Meacham begat Daphne Meacham. Daphne Meacham begat Fred Taylor, and so on.

DUD. Course you can trace it all back to Adam and Eve.

PETE. The first two.

DUD. Yer, they were the first two. But what I don't understand, Pete, is how two people produced so many millions of different colour, kith, race and creed.

PETE. You mean how did Adam and Eve have all these children of myriad hues?

DUD. Yer.

PETE. Well, the point of that, Dud, is that Genesis isn't true in the literal sense, it's an allergy. Genesis is an allergy of *la condition humaine*, it's about the whole lot of the human race. Adam and Eve aren't just Adam and Eve, they're the whole human race personified. Do you believe in God, actually?

DUD. I tell you Pete, when I'm in a tight spot I say to myself, 'God please help me out, if You're there. If You do help me out, I'll believe in You and thank You very much. I'll know You're there for future reference.'

PETE. Yer, I have a similar attitude. Whenever I feel ill, you know, I get a dose of the flu or something, I say a little prayer. I say, 'Dear God in heaven, if You're there, heed my prayer. If You're not there, don't take any notice. But if You are, make me better by Tuesday at twelve o'clock and I'll know You've done it, and I promise to be good for ever more and believe in You.' Of course the trouble is, when you get better you don't know whether it's because God's done it or whether you would have got better in any case. There's no real way of telling what He's up to or even where He is.

DUD. No, you can't tell, can you really.

PETE. I often wish He'd manifest himself a bit more, you know, in the sky.

DUD. Yer, it'd be nice if every now and again He parted the clouds and in a golden burst of sunshine gave you a wave. 'Hello down there, you can believe in me.'

PETE. I asked the Reverend Stephens about this, and he said, 'Much as God would like to keep manifesting Himself, He daren't, you see, because it debases the currency.' He can't go round all the football matches and fêtes and everything, so He limits himself to once in a million years if we're lucky.

DUD. Well, you've got to be careful about over-exposure. Course you know, actually, Pete, I wish I'd never been told about God at all 'cause it means we can't get away with nothing, doesn't it? I mean you've been told about Him, you know He's there or you think He's there, and you can't really mess about then, can you?

PETE. You can't.

DUD. No, and what about the people who haven't been told about God?

PETE. Well, I asked the Reverend Stephens this, and he said that if you haven't been told about God, Dud, you're laughing. If you don't know good from evil then you're away. You can do anything you bloody well like. There's these people in New Guinea for example. They wander about with nothing on and they commit adultery, steal, and covet their neighbour's wife, which everyone wants to do. As there are no vicars about, to tell them everything, they can't be got at, so they go up to heaven whatever they do. This means all these nig-nogs are getting up to heaven, and perfectly decent blokes like you and me, who have never even committed adultery, we can't get up there. We're being kept out by these Guineans.

DUD. You see in that case, Pete, it'd be a crime to tell people about God.

PETE. I've never told anyone about God.

DUD. I haven't told anyone, I haven't mentioned it to a soul, Pete.

PETE. St Paul's got a bloody lot to answer for.

DUD. He started it didn't he – all those letters he wrote.

PETE. To the Ephiscans.

DUD. You know, 'Dear Ephiscans, Stop enjoying yourself, God's about the place. Signed Paul.'

PETE. You can just imagine it, can't you. There's a nice Ephiscan family settling down to a good breakfast of fried mussels and hot coffee and just sitting there. It's a lovely day outside and they're thinking of taking the children out for picnic by the sea and everything's happy and the sun's coming through the trees, birds are chirping away.

DUD. The distant cry of happy children, and clouds scudding across the sky.

PETE. In fact an idyllic scene is what you'd call it, an idyllic scene. When suddenly into the midst of it all – tap, tap, on the bloody door. You know who it is?

DUD. No.

PETE. It's a messenger bearing a letter from Paul.

DUD. Dad runs to the door to open it, thinking it may be good news,

PETE. Perhaps Grandfather's died and left them the vineyards.

DUD. They open it up and what do they discover?

PETE. 'Dear George and Deirdre and Family, Stop having a good time, resign yourself to not having a picnic, cover yourself with ashes and start flaying yourselves, until further notice, Signed Paul.'

DUD. A dreadful sort of letter to get, isn't it?

PETE. Terrible.

DUD. Course, you know, actually I'm fascinated by those religions which say you come back in a different form.

PETE. Reincarnation.

DUD. Reincarnation.

PETE. Yer. Buddhists believe in that, coming back as a different creature of some kind or other.

DUD. What would *you* come back as?

PETE. Well, I think if I had a choice, I'd probably come back as a royal corgi and go sniffing about the Palace, you know.

DUD. That's very good, actually, improve your station.

PETE. Course you could come back as something terrible, couldn't you.

DUD. Well, suppose you came back as a humble mayfly.

PETE. Well, of course you'd only live for six hours wouldn't you. They have a very futile life, them mayflies, they only live six hours. As soon as they're born, they're worried about old age. By the time they're three hours old they're really middle aged, they can't run for buses like they used to. They got grey hairs all over their legs, and in another three hours they're gaga and they die.

DUD. Terrible business.

PETE. You know Mr Thomas.

DUD. Yer.

PETE. Next door.

DUD. Yer.

PETE. He's a Buddhist.

DUD. He's not.

PETE. Yer, he's a Buddhist.

DUD. Is he really?

PETE. Yer, he's a Buddhist. He's got this bluebottle in the bathroom. He thinks it's Keats. He thinks it's the poet Keats reincarnated, so he keeps going into the bathroom, takes it in marshmallows and marmalade. The bluebottle's getting very fat, terrible great thing. He puts out bits of paper, hoping he'll complete some poems. He's just got a lot of bluebottle droppings so far. He still frames them, though.

DUD. They'd probably mean something to another bluebottle.

PETE. Well, true bluebottles would understand it wouldn't they.

DUD. Course actually I'd like to come back as a sparrow so I could see down ladies' blouses.

PETE. There wouldn't be much point in that, Dud. If you came back as a sparrow, you wouldn't want to look down ladies' blouses.

DUD. No, you'd just want to look down sparrows' blouses.

PETE. You'd be interested in them – as a sparrow. If I had my choice I'd like to come back as Grace Kelly.

DUD. Why's that?

PETE. I've always wanted to know what she looks like in the bath. I've always been fascinated by her glacial beauty.

DUD. Course, actually, you know, Pete, in the end, it's a bit of a toss-up as to which religion is right, isn't it? You can't actually know which religion is right.

PETE. No, you can't tell. There are millions of religions. It might be Buddhism, it might be Christianity.

DUD. You don't know what to go for, do you, actually?

PETE. No, you might be a perfectly good Buddhist all your life, get up to heaven and there will be the Reverend Stephens saying, 'Get out, ha, ha ha,

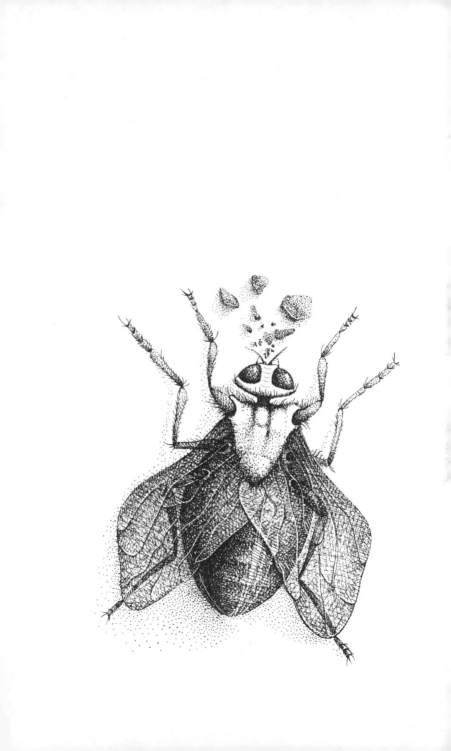

Buddhism is wrong. We're right! Buddha off!'

DUD. Alternatively you might be a very good Christian, Church of England, behave yourself very nicely, get up there and there's Buddha –

PETE. Laughing all over his face and sends you back as a worm.

DUD. I think the best thing is to remain a prognostic.

PETE. An agnostic.

DUD. Do you think God's been listening while we've been talking?

PETE. Well, if He exists, He's been listening because He's omnipresent. He's heard every word we've said.

DUD. Oh, we'd better look religious, then.

PETE. It's no good just looking religious Dud, He can see through that. You have to *be* religious. What do you *really* believe in?

DUD. I believe in having a good time. Food and kip and Joan Whittaker and that.

PETE. That's not religion, Dud. That's Hedonism. You're a Heddist.

DUD. No, I'm a Duddist. That's what I call it.